PARALLEL LIVES

ANNE FRANK

Born in 1929

MARTIN LUTHER KING JR.

Julie Knutson

CHERRY LAKE PRESS

Published in the United States of America by Cherry Lake Publishing
Ann Arbor, Michigan
www.cherrylakepublishing.com

Reading Adviser: Marla Conn, MS, Ed., Literacy specialist, Read-Ability, Inc.
Cover Designer: Felicia Macheske

Photo Credits: © Courtesy Anne Frank House, cover, 1 [left]; © Library of Congress/Dick Demarsico, photographer, 1964/www.loc.gov/item/00651714, cover, 2 [right]; © Library of Congress, LC-DIG-fsa-8b38283, 5; © Everett Historical/Shutterstock.com, 6; © Library of Congress, 3c30357u, 7; © Library of Congress, LC-DIG-ppmsca-38818, 8; © hans engbers/Shutterstock.com, 11; © World History Archive/Alamy Stock Photo, 12; © Alatom/iStock.com, 14; © Courtesy Anne Frank House, 16; © Library of Congress, LC-USZ62-122986, 19; © Forty3Zero/Shutterstock.com, 21; © Library of Congress, LC-DIG-ds-06479, 22; © Library of Congress, LC-DIG-ppmsca-47100, 24; © Library of Congress, LC-USZ62-111165, 25; © CNP/Getty Images, 26

Library of Congress Cataloging-in-Publication Data

Names: Knutson, Julie, author.
Title: Born in 1929 : Anne Frank and Martin Luther King, Jr. / by Julie Knutson.
Other titles: Anne Frank and Martin Luther King, Jr.
Description: Ann Arbor, Michigan : Cherry Lake Publishing, [2020] | Series: Parallel lives | Includes index. | Audience: Grades 4-6
Identifiers: LCCN 2019033480 (print) | LCCN 2019033481 (ebook) | ISBN 9781534159174 (hardcover) | ISBN 9781534161474 (paperback) | ISBN 9781534162624 (ebook) | ISBN 9781534160323 (PDF)
Subjects: LCSH: Human rights workers—Biography—Juvenile literature. | Civil rights workers—Biography—Juvenile literature. | Frank, Anne, 1929-1945—Juvenile literature. | Jewish children in the Holocaust—Netherlands—Amsterdam—Biography—Juvenile literature. | Diarists—Netherlands—Amsterdam—Biography—Juvenile literature. | King, Martin Luther, Jr., 1929-1968—Juvenile literature. | African American civil rights workers—Alabama—Biography—Juvenile literature.
Classification: LCC JC571 .B667 2020 (print) | LCC JC571 (ebook) | DDC 323.092 [B]—dc23
LC record available at https://lccn.loc.gov/2019033480
LC ebook record available at https://lccn.loc.gov/2019033481

Cherry Lake Publishing would like to acknowledge the work of the Partnership for 21st Century Learning, a Network of Battelle for Kids. Please visit www.battelleforkids.org/networks/p21 for more information.

Printed in the United States of America
Corporate Graphics

ABOUT THE AUTHOR

Julie Knutson shares a birth year with Venus Williams, Chelsea Clinton, and Lin-Manuel Miranda. An avid student of history and former teacher, she lives in northern Illinois with her husband and son.

TABLE OF CONTENTS

CHAPTER 1

Welcome to 1929

1929. Two people with a shared belief in the power of words—Anne Frank and Martin Luther King Jr.—are born an ocean apart. The world into which they arrived was in turmoil. On October 28, the stock market crashed, launching a 10-year period of global economic instability known as the **Great Depression**. People in Europe and the United States blamed losing their fortunes on minority groups.

The Rise of the Nazi Party in Germany: In the decade that followed Germany's loss in World War I (1914–1918), the country suffered economic and political distress. Adolf Hitler looked to capitalize on the unhappiness of the German people. Hitler led the National-Socialist German Workers' Party (Nazi Party),

A series of dust storms ravaged the United States during the 1930s.

The swastika symbol originally meant good luck.
However, the Nazi Party turned it into a symbol of hate.

which blamed the country's Jewish population and other minorities for Germany's misfortunes. As the Great Depression set in during the early 1930s, the party's **anti-Semitic** platform gained more support. On January 30, 1933, Hitler was sworn in as Germany's **chancellor**.

Segregation and "Jim Crow" Laws in the United States: **Jim Crow laws** allowed for legal **segregation** in many parts of the United States starting in the late 1800s. In 1929, black students had to attend separate schools, drink from separate water fountains,

In the case of *Plessy v. Ferguson* (1896), the U.S. Supreme Court ruled that "separate but equal" facilities were legal.

The NAACP was founded in 1909 by a group of prominent African American figures like W. E. B. Du Bois and Ida B. Wells.

and sit in separate balconies of movie theaters. Restaurants and shops—especially in the South—frequently refused to serve black customers. Under legal segregation, African Americans were also denied educational and employment opportunities. Groups like the National Association for the Advancement of Colored People (NAACP) and the Urban League worked to dismantle segregation and establish **civil rights** for all Americans.

The Nuremberg Laws of 1935

*In September 1935, Hitler's government introduced the Nuremberg Laws. These laws stripped German Jews of their citizenship rights, labeling them "state subjects." German Jews could no longer marry non-Jews or work in certain professions. In November 1935, the laws were expanded to include the country's **Romani** and black populations.*

CHAPTER 2

Anne Frank

(b. June 12, 1929)

From June 1942 until August 1944, Anne Frank poured her thoughts onto the pages of her journal, which she named "Kitty." Anne's diary begins on her 13th birthday, June 12, 1942. Less than 1 month later, her Jewish family took refuge with others in a secret **annex** to escape Nazi capture. Eight people hid together in a small apartment. While there, Anne used writing to "record everything, all my thoughts, my ideals, and my fantasies." Found and published after her death, the diary has now been translated into 70 languages, allowing Anne's voice to live on around the world for more than 70 years.

The Diary of Anne Frank is often assigned reading
in classrooms across the United States.

On November 9, 1938, German Nazis attacked Jewish businesses and homes. This night is referred to as *Kristallnacht*, or the Night of Broken Glass.

Early Years: Finding a Voice

Anne was born in Frankfurt, Germany. Her father, Otto, was a successful businessman. Her mother, Edith, cared for Anne and her older sister, Margot, with the help of a nanny. The social and political climate in Frankfurt, as in all of Germany, worsened for Jews in the late 1920s and early 1930s. Before Anne's second birthday, the Frank family was pressured into moving to another area within the city on account of their Jewish heritage. However, they were soon forced to flee the country altogether, as anti-Semitism continued to mount with the rise of Adolf Hitler. They first sought refuge in Switzerland before moving to Amsterdam in 1934.

Anne and Margot quickly adjusted to life in Amsterdam, a city known for being inclusive and tolerant. They learned Dutch and attended school with non-Jewish peers. Anne was a mischievous, popular girl who loved a good prank. She liked to skate on frozen

Resistance

In France, Italy, and the Netherlands, Jews and non-Jews alike fought back against Nazi forces. On February 25, 1941, Amsterdam's working class ordered a general strike. It was organized by leftist groups, who issued the call, "Strike! Strike! Strike! Shut down all of Amsterdam for a day!" Streetcar drivers and garbage collectors stopped working. They were followed by dockworkers and drivers. Across the city, everything closed—factories, offices, shops, and restaurants. It is believed that around 300,000 people took part. In the days that followed, the strike spread to the nearby towns of Haarlem and Utrecht.

*German forces were unprepared for a strike of this size, but they soon fought back. Many strikers were arrested and injured, and nine were killed. February 25 is still celebrated in the Netherlands as a day honoring anti-***Fascist*** resistance.*

The first Nazi concentration camps opened in 1933.
Originally, they held political prisoners.

canals in the winter and swim in the North Sea during the
summer. But that all changed in May 1940. The Nazi policies that
the Franks fled in Germany arrived in Amsterdam when the
Germans bombed and took over the city. On February 22, 1941,
Nazi troops rounded up hundreds of the city's Jews and sent them
to **concentration camps**. New laws and rules were put into
place. Jewish students had to attend separate schools. Jewish
residents were banned from beaches, pools, museums, restaurants,
and libraries. By April 1942, extreme laws restricting Jewish
movement and behaviors such as riding bikes, driving cars, or
being out past a certain time, were in place.

Middle Years: Expressing a Voice

By the summer of 1942, it was too late for Anne's family to flee the country. The only option was to hide. For months, Otto and Edith had moved furniture and belongings into a secret annex above his office. The Franks hurriedly moved in on July 6, 1942, after Margot received a letter that ordered her to report to a labor camp. The cramped space offered little-to-no privacy, and they had to be totally silent during the day. For Anne, who often quarreled with her mother and sister, her diary provided a place to be expressive, understood, and unjudged.

On April 11, 1944, Anne wrote, "If God lets me live ... I'll make my voice heard, I'll go out into the world and work for mankind." Less than 4 months later, the Franks' hiding place was uncovered. The eight residents of the secret annex were arrested. The Frank family was transported first to the concentration camp Westerbork and then to Auschwitz. Anne and Margot were later separated from their parents and sent to Bergen-Belsen. At this point in the war, the Nazis were executing up to 6,000 people a day at Auschwitz and Bergen-Belsen. Sometime between February and March of 1945, Anne died of typhus, a disease that spreads through overcrowding and poor living conditions. In April, the camp was set free by British troops.

The Anne Frank House, turned into a museum in 1960, welcomes over a million visitors a year.

Later Years: Leaving a Legacy

Anne's father, Otto, was the only member of the Frank family to survive the war. His assistant, Miep Gies, had rescued Anne's diary from the annex and kept it in a drawer. Otto read the journal as he recovered. He felt his teenage daughter return to life through its pages. In 1947, he shared the diary with the world. It personalizes the more than 6 million lives lost in the Holocaust, and stands as a lasting reminder of the human cost of war. Through this document, Anne's voice remains heard, and her words continue to urge humankind toward a more just future.

Our Evolving Understanding of Anne

Versions of Anne Frank's diary have changed over time. In the first publication in 1947, her father edited out certain details that he felt were too personal. These details were reintroduced in later editions. In more recent years, additional pages have been discovered. In 2016, researchers uncovered two pages previously concealed by brown adhesive paper.

CHAPTER 3

Martin Luther King Jr.
(b. January 15, 1929)

Civil rights organizer and activist Martin Luther King Jr. raised his voice—never his fists—against racial and economic **injustice**. With words and nonviolent protest, he inspired a movement to make the United States do right on its promise of "liberty and justice for all."

Early Years: Finding a Voice

Martin was born on January 15, 1929, in Atlanta, Georgia. His father was a minister and community leader. Martin's mother, Alberta, was a college-educated woman known for her kind, easygoing manner. In the King household, social justice was a frequent topic of conversation. When young Martin faced **discrimination**, he reflected on it—whether it came from a white neighbor who no longer wanted to play with him because of his race, or a business

Martin Luther King Jr. received the Nobel Peace Prize in 1964.

owner who refused the family service. His parents nurtured this reflection and supported his interest in speaking out against prejudice.

Martin was an outstanding student. He graduated from high school at age 15 and went on to Morehouse College. There, he read the writings of different philosophers, which influenced his arguments against racism. One philosopher was Henry David Thoreau, who promoted the idea of **civil disobedience**. Thoreau, who lived in the mid-1800s, believed that people should disobey unjust laws. Martin later wrote, "Fascinated by the idea of refusing to cooperate with an evil system, I was so deeply moved that I reread the work several times. I became so convinced that noncooperation with evil is as much a moral obligation as is cooperation with good." Martin went on to attend school in Boston, Massachusetts, where he paired Thoreau's thoughts with the actions of leaders like Mahatma Gandhi. These two figures provided the intellectual basis and model of action that the young activist needed to build a movement.

Gandhi and Nonviolence

Mohandas "Mahatma" Gandhi led the movement for Indian independence from British rule in the mid-1900s. He did so through nonviolent actions like protest marches, hunger strikes, and boycotts. His efforts inspired activists seeking freedom and justice around the world, including in the United States.

The Martin Luther King Jr. Memorial Mural in Atlanta, Georgia,
features King and other important civil rights leaders.

Coretta Scott King was equally passionate about the civil rights movement. She gave speeches, held events, and continued to campaign after her husband's death.

Middle Years: Expressing a Voice

Martin developed his leadership and public speaking skills while a student of **theology**. As he prepared to enter the ministry, he and his wife, Coretta, had to decide where they would live. Martin was offered jobs in Massachusetts, New York, and Montgomery, Alabama. It was 1954, and the South was still very segregated. Should the young couple settle in the North, which was generally more welcoming to African Americans? Or should he begin his professional life in the South, fighting injustice? Martin and Coretta chose Montgomery. In his early sermons,

The Poor People's Campaign

On December 4, 1967, King announced a new cause, called the Poor People's Campaign. A **coalition** of more than 50 organizations representing all races **lobbied** for equal education and employment, fair wages, and better housing. They asked the U.S. government to set aside $30 billion each year for these issues. They also pressed for a guaranteed national income and affordable housing.

Organizers mapped three phases to the campaign. First, a **shantytown** would be constructed on the National Mall in Washington, D.C. Second, protesters would occupy this camp, educating the public and Congress on the effects of poverty and needed reforms. This phase would be followed by mass, nonviolent protests and boycotts to draw attention to their demands.

Martin Luther King Jr. died before the campaign began in May 1968. Organizers honored his vision by launching the first phase of the campaign. About 3,000 protesters lived in the shantytown known as "Resurrection City" that spring and summer. An additional 50,000 people gathered to protest for economic justice on the National Mall on June 19, 1968. And while the campaign's goals still haven't been met today, there's a renewed effort to address them. A 21st-century Poor People's Campaign is focused on raising the minimum wage.

Rosa Parks was actually sitting in the "colored section" when she was asked to give up her seat.

he encouraged people to get involved in politics by registering to vote and supporting NAACP efforts.

By late 1955, Martin had built arguments against segregation, developed nonviolent approaches, organized activist networks, and spoken out against prejudice. These efforts inspired others and helped spark a movement. On December 1, Rosa Parks, an African American resident of Montgomery, refused to give her bus seat to a white passenger. She was arrested. In response, Martin and other community leaders organized a **boycott**. African Americans in the city refused to use the city's bus system in their push for

At 26 years old, Martin Luther King Jr. was elected president of the Montgomery Improvement Association (MIA).

Martin's "I Have a Dream" speech was delivered
at the Lincoln Memorial in Washington, D.C.

desegregation. Protesters, including Martin, endured physical
violence, countless attacks, and unjust arrests. But after 381 days,
buses were desegregated. With support from the Supreme Court,
the civil rights movement earned a major victory.

Throughout the 1950s and 1960s, Martin organized and inspired
boycotts, marches, speeches, and strikes in Washington, D.C.,
Birmingham and Selma, Alabama, and Atlanta, Georgia. He helped
launch the Southern Christian Leadership Conference (SCLC) in

1957, which earned major victories by successfully lobbying Congress to pass the Civil Rights Act of 1964 and Voting Rights Act of 1965. Their work showed that nonviolent action could—and did—lead to social, political, and economic changes that supported the human rights of all.

Later Years: Leaving a Legacy

On April 4, 1968, Martin was fatally shot in Memphis, Tennessee. His words—from his "I Have a Dream" speech to his "Letters from a Birmingham Jail"—continue to inspire civil disobedience and nonviolent resistance. The actions and protests he organized provided a model for other activists in the United States and beyond, from farmworkers to the LGBTQ community. Today, he's celebrated as an American icon who fought tirelessly and sacrificed his life for the causes of racial and economic justice.

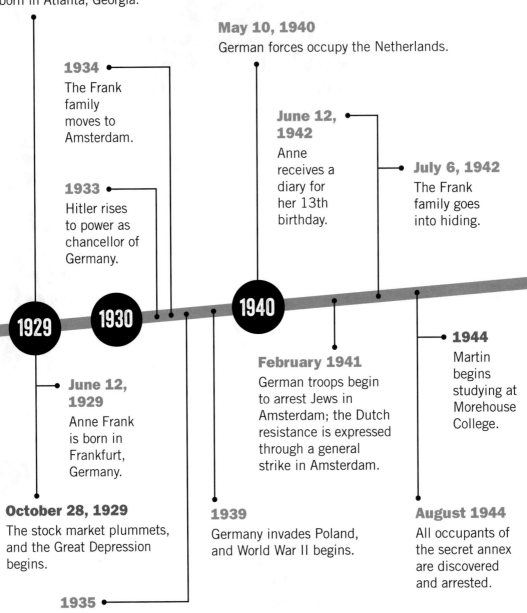

January 15, 1929
Martin Luther King Jr. is born in Atlanta, Georgia.

May 10, 1940
German forces occupy the Netherlands.

1934
The Frank family moves to Amsterdam.

June 12, 1942
Anne receives a diary for her 13th birthday.

July 6, 1942
The Frank family goes into hiding.

1933
Hitler rises to power as chancellor of Germany.

1929

1930

1940

June 12, 1929
Anne Frank is born in Frankfurt, Germany.

February 1941
German troops begin to arrest Jews in Amsterdam; the Dutch resistance is expressed through a general strike in Amsterdam.

1944
Martin begins studying at Morehouse College.

October 28, 1929
The stock market plummets, and the Great Depression begins.

1939
Germany invades Poland, and World War II begins.

August 1944
All occupants of the secret annex are discovered and arrested.

1935
Nuremberg Laws take effect, stripping German Jews of citizenship rights.

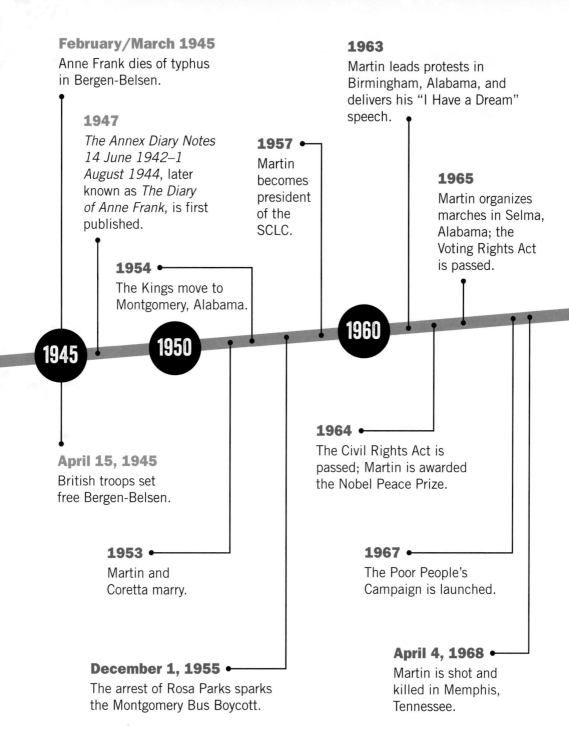

February/March 1945
Anne Frank dies of typhus in Bergen-Belsen.

1947
The Annex Diary Notes 14 June 1942–1 August 1944, later known as *The Diary of Anne Frank*, is first published.

1954
The Kings move to Montgomery, Alabama.

1945

April 15, 1945
British troops set free Bergen-Belsen.

1953
Martin and Coretta marry.

December 1, 1955
The arrest of Rosa Parks sparks the Montgomery Bus Boycott.

1957
Martin becomes president of the SCLC.

1963
Martin leads protests in Birmingham, Alabama, and delivers his "I Have a Dream" speech.

1965
Martin organizes marches in Selma, Alabama; the Voting Rights Act is passed.

1950

1960

1964
The Civil Rights Act is passed; Martin is awarded the Nobel Peace Prize.

1967
The Poor People's Campaign is launched.

April 4, 1968
Martin is shot and killed in Memphis, Tennessee.

Research and Act

At the end of Martin Luther King Jr.'s life, his focus was on poverty.
Economic inequality often affects people of color and marginalized groups.
Systematic racism is often at the root of the issue. How do we overcome it?

Research
Research poverty today in your community and beyond. What is the poverty rate in your city or town? In the United States? Globally? What conditions cause poverty? How are people addressing it locally and globally? How can you get involved?

Act
Work together with family and friends to address economic inequality in your community. Organize a volunteer day at a local soup kitchen or homeless shelter. Plan a school clothing or food drive for people in need. The opportunities are endless! You too can make a difference.

Further Reading

Bader, Bonnie. *Who Was Martin Luther King Jr.?* New York, NY: Grosset & Dunlap, 2008.

Calkhoven, Laurie. *Martin Luther King Jr.* New York, NY: DK Publishing, 2019.

Cooke, Tim. *Anne Frank*. New York, NY: Gareth Stevens Publishing, 2019.

Fishman, Jon M. *Martin Luther King Jr.: Walking in the Light*. Minneapolis, MN: Lerner Publications, 2019.

Frank, Anne. *The Diary of Anne Frank: The Revised Critical Edition*. New York, NY: Doubleday, 2003.

Krensky, Stephen. *Anne Frank*. New York, NY: DK Publishing, 2019.

GLOSSARY

annex (AN-eks) an extra room or space attached to a main building

anti-Semitic (an-tee-suh-MIH-tik) hostility toward or bias against Jewish people

boycott (BOI-kaht) a refusal by people to do business with others as a form of protest

chancellor (CHAN-suh-lur) head of state

civil disobedience (SIV-uhl dis-uh-BEE-dee-uhns) refusal to follow certain laws, rules, or practices as a form of peaceful protest

civil rights (SIV-uhl RITES) rights to political and social freedom, regardless of race, gender, or social class

coalition (koh-uh-LISH-uhn) group of people who organize around a shared belief, movement, or cause

concentration camps (kahn-suhn-TRAY-shuhn KAMPS) places where people were forced to live under horrible conditions

discrimination (dis-krim-ih-NAY-shuhn) unfair behavior to others based on differences in race or gender

economic inequality (ee-kuh-NAH-mik in-ih-KWAH-lih-tee) the unequal distribution of income and opportunity between different groups in society

Fascist (FASH-ist) political philosophy that endorses a strong central government with no tolerance for opposing viewpoints

Great Depression (GRAYT dih-PRESH-uhn) period of global economic stress spanning from 1929 to 1939

injustice (in-JUHS-tis) an unfair situation or action

Jim Crow laws (JIM KROH LAWZ) laws in many U.S. states that set different rules for black and white Americans, in effect from the late-19th to mid-20th centuries

lobbied (LAH-beed) worked to influence someone about a specific political issue

Romani (roh-MAH-nee) an ethnic group sometimes referred to as "gypsies"

segregation (seg-rih-GAY-shuhn) the practice of keeping people or groups (such as racial or ethnic) apart

shantytown (SHAN-tee-toun) temporary camp or settlement

systematic racism (sis-tuh-MAT-ik RAY-siz-uhm) laws or policies in place that negatively impact the advancement of minorities

theology (thee-AH-luh-jee) study of God and religion

INDEX